8-4-99

D0611611

# May I Quote You, Stonewall Jackson?

# MAY I QUOTE YOU, STONEWALL JACKSON?

*Observations and Utterances of the South's Great Generals*

Randall Bedwell

CUMBERLAND HOUSE

PUBLISHING INC.

Some quotes have been edited for clarity and brevity.

Managing Editor: Carol Boker
Associate Editor: Hollis Dodge
Contributing Editors: Palmer Jones, Jim Vaden, Debbie Petite
Historical Advisors: Edward F. Williams III, Jim Fox

Typography: The BookSetters Co.
Text design: The BookSetters Co.
Cover design: Patterson Graham Design Group

Library of Congress Cataloging-in-Publication Data
May I quote you, Stonewall Jackson? : observations and utterances of the
  South's great generals / [compiled by] Randall Bedwell.
    p.  cm.  —(May I quote you, General? series)
  ISBN 1-888952-36-9 (pbk. : alk. paper)
  1. Jackson, Stonewall, 1824-1863—Quotations.  2. United States—
History—Civil War, 1861-1865—Quotations, maxims, etc.  3. Quotations,
American.  I. Bedwell, Randall J.  II. Series.
E467.1.J15M39  1997
973.7'3'092—dc21                                          96-52697
                                                            CIP

Printed in the United States of America
2  3  4  5  6  7  8—01  00  99  98  97

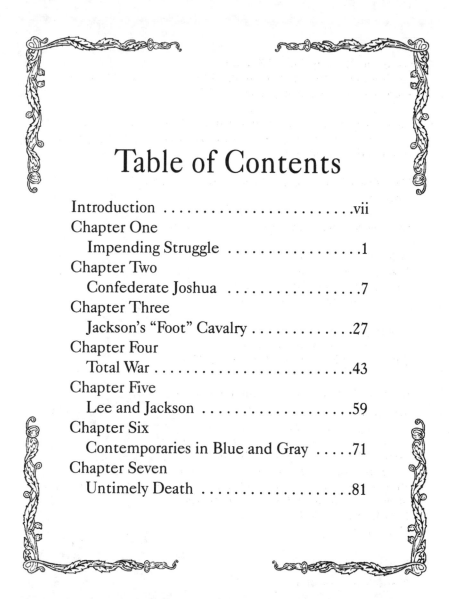

# Table of Contents

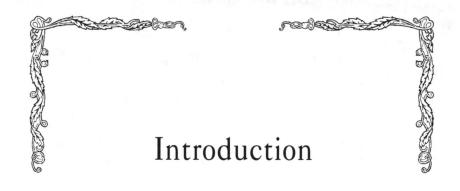

# Introduction

General Thomas J. "Stonewall" Jackson's untimely death by "friendly fire" at Chancellorsville dealt a crushing blow to the hopes of the Confederacy. The Rebel armies' reputation for consistently defeating their enemy's numerically superior forces was in large part due to Jackson's exploits in the Shenandoah Valley Campaign. Stonewall's threat to the federal capitol first demonstrated his talent for forced marches and pitched battles.

By the time he reached the pinnacle of his military career, Jackson had found his ideal fighting ally in General Robert E. Lee. The two formed a near-invincible team as leaders of the Army of Northern

Virginia. After Chancellorsville, however, Lee never again saw his army execute battle plans to the same level of perfection as when his ablest lieutenant was there to lend his abilities and judgment. Indeed, the revered Lee went so far as to claim a Confederate victory would have occurred had it not been for Jackson's fatal reconnaissance: "He never failed me. Why, if I had had Stonewall Jackson at Gettysburg, I should have won that battle: and a complete victory would have . . . established the independence of the Confederacy."

*May I Quote You, Stonewall Jackson?* celebrates the wisdom and determination of one of the South's most unique and idiosyncratic commanders. A figure truly commensurate with the war's epic scope, Stonewall Jackson's words capture the era in all its glory and sorrow.

*Randall Bedwell*
*Cordova, Tennessee*
*September 1996*

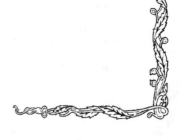

CHAPTER ONE

# Impending Struggle

Inevitable war loomed heavily upon the nation by 1860. Haunted by decades of dissension over slavery, and apprehension about the results of the presidential election, the country began to divide with the secession of South Carolina from the Union.

Motivated by loyalty to their homeland and the desire to defend it, men began to take sides. One such soldier, Thomas Jonathan Jackson, was summoned to lead his Virginia brigade. For thirty-seven years, Jackson had unknowingly prepared for this duty as well as any man can prepare for the inconceivable task of fighting one's countrymen. Battles in Mexico had taught him military strategies, orderliness, discipline, and devotion, and established him as the "fighting man." Jackson was ready, and he devoted himself to the Confederate cause. It was a dedication that consumed him for twenty-three months until the end of his life

People who are anxious to bring on war don't know what they are bargaining for; they don't see all the horrors that must accompany such an event.

—*Stonewall Jackson*

I am in favor of making a thorough trial for peace, and if we fail in this and our state is invaded, to defend it with terrific resistance.

—*Stonewall Jackson to his nephew, January 1861*

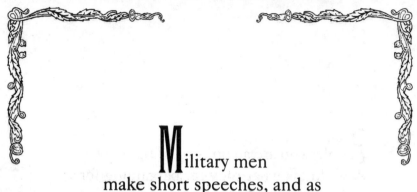

**M**ilitary men
make short speeches, and as
for myself I am no hand at speaking
anyhow. The time for war has not yet
come, but it will come, and that soon;
and when it does come, my advice is
to draw the sword and throw
away the scabbard.

—*Professor Thomas J. Jackson*
*to Virginia Military Institute cadets,*
*April 13, 1861*

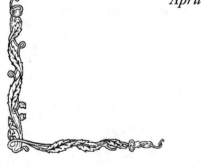

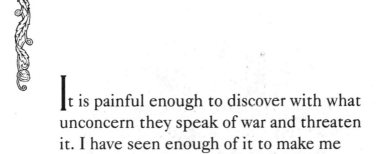

It is painful enough to discover with what unconcern they speak of war and threaten it. I have seen enough of it to make me look upon it as the sum of all evils.

—*Stonewall Jackson, 1861*

All I am and all I have is at the service of my country.

—*Stonewall Jackson, 1861*

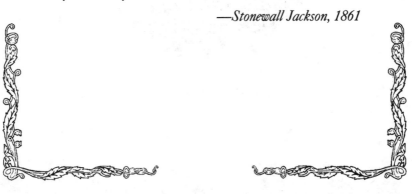

Stonewall Jackson

# CHAPTER TWO

# Confederate Joshua

A dynamic warrior in Biblical times, Joshua led Israel in the conquest of Canaan, vanquishing Jericho and other cities to bring Palestine under Israelite control. Joshua's leadership, with the divine guidance of God, was marked by courage and devotion to the law given to Moses.

In the Civil War, another brave warrior felt he was similarly led by Providence. Thomas "Stonewall" Jackson believed he was God's instrument on Earth, and God was watching his every move. His mission was victory for the Almighty. To Jackson, there were no shades of gray: You either obeyed or disobeyed; you were either a God-fearing man or you were not. Through his strong faith, he reinforced the resolve and beliefs of fellow Southerners as he shepherded his followers into battle.

Our God was my shield. His protecting care is an additional cause for gratitude.

*—Stonewall Jackson, Winchester, 1862*

I am truly grateful to the Giver of Victory for having blessed us in our terrible struggle. I pray He may continue.

*—Robert E. Lee to Stonewall Jackson, 1862*

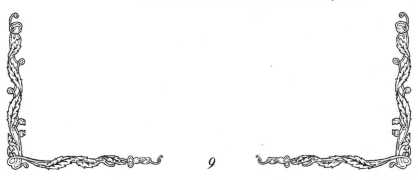

So far as I can see, my course was a wise one; the best that I could do under the circumstances, though very distasteful to my feelings; and I hope and pray to Our Heavenly Father that I may never again be circumstanced as on that day.

—*Stonewall Jackson after fighting a battle on Sunday, Winchester, 1862*

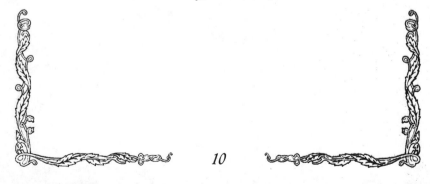

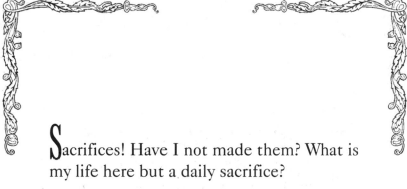

**S**acrifices! Have I not made them? What is my life here but a daily sacrifice?

*—Stonewall Jackson, in a resignation letter
that was never acted upon, 1862*

**I**f you desire to be more heavenly minded, think more of the things of heaven, and less of the things of earth.

*—Stonewall Jackson*

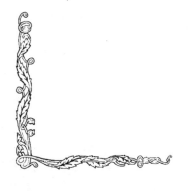
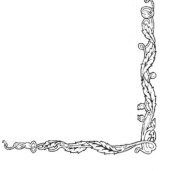

No, you greatly overestimate my capacity for usefulness. A better man will soon be sent to take my place.

*—Stonewall Jackson, 1861*

My religious belief teaches me to feel as safe in battle as in bed. God has fixed the time for my death. I do not concern myself about that, but to always be ready, no matter when it may overtake me.

*—Stonewall Jackson*

If we cannot be
successful in defeating
the enemy should he advance,
a kind Providence may enable us
to inflict a terrible wound and
effect a safe retreat in the
event of having to
fall back.

—*Stonewall Jackson to Joseph E. Johnston, 1862*

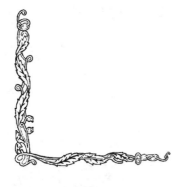
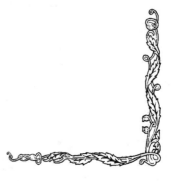

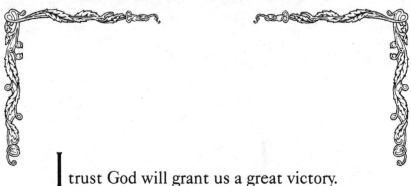

I trust God will grant us a great victory.

*—Stonewall Jackson to J. E. B. Stuart*
*before Chancellorsville, May 1, 1863*

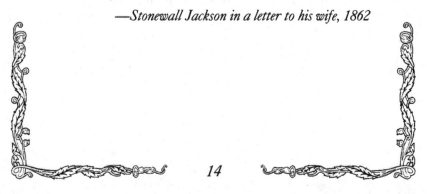

Our gallant little army is increasing in numbers, and my prayer is that it may be an army of the living God as well as of its country.

*—Stonewall Jackson in a letter to his wife, 1862*

The future of our ancestors belongs only to them. It is up to us to make our own future.

*—Stonewall Jackson*

Through life let your principal object be the discharge of duty.

*—Stonewall Jackson*

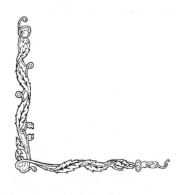
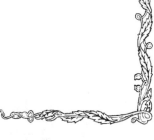

**R**esolve
to perform what
you ought; perform
without fail what
you resolve.

—*Stonewall Jackson*

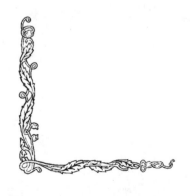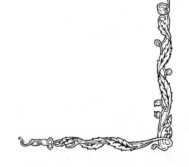

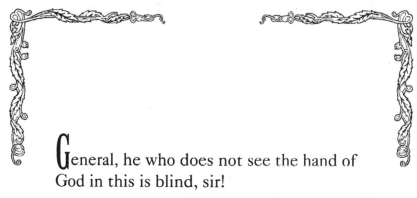

General, he who does not see the hand of God in this is blind, sir!

*—Stonewall Jackson to Ewell at Port Republic*

You may be whatever you resolve to be.

*—Stonewall Jackson*

Never take counsel of your fears.

*—Stonewall Jackson*

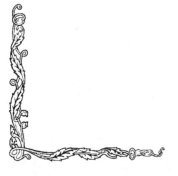

Ⅼod has been our shield, and to His name be all the glory. . . . How do I wish for peace, but only upon the condition of our national independence!

*—Stonewall Jackson to his wife, Anna, after his Valley Campaign in 1862*

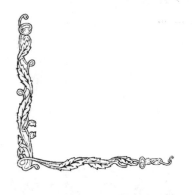
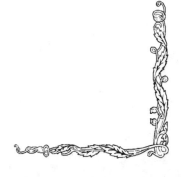

The Lord has answered our prayers; He has again placed us across Bull Run; and I pray that He will make our aims entirely satisfactory. . . . God has blessed and preserved me through His great mercy.

*—Stonewall Jackson to his wife after Second Manassas*

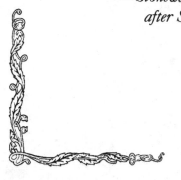

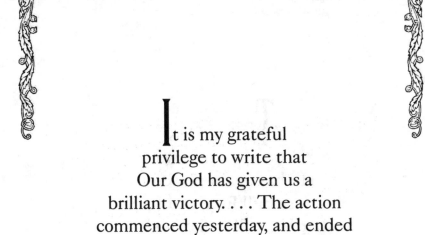

It is my grateful privilege to write that Our God has given us a brilliant victory. . . . The action commenced yesterday, and ended this morning in capitulation. Our Heavenly Father blesses us exceedingly.

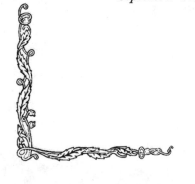

—*Stonewall Jackson to his wife, dated September 15, after Harper's Ferry*

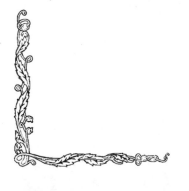

I would like to see no questions asked in the army as to what denomination a chaplain belongs; but let the question be, Does he preach the Gospel?

*—General Thomas J. Jackson, 1863*

I knew that what I *willed* to do, I *could* do.

*—Stonewall Jackson on his appointment as professor at VMI*

Yes, God
blessed our army
again yesterday, and I
hope with His protection
and blessing we shall
do still better
today.

—*Stonewall Jackson after Cross Keys*

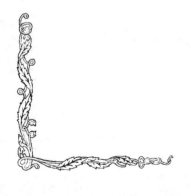
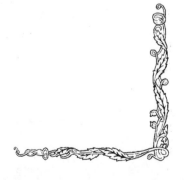

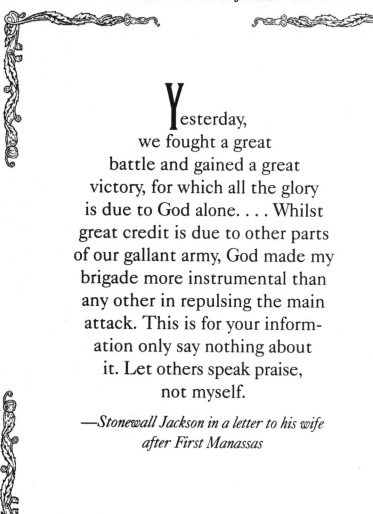

Yesterday,
we fought a great
battle and gained a great
victory, for which all the glory
is due to God alone. . . . Whilst
great credit is due to other parts
of our gallant army, God made my
brigade more instrumental than
any other in repulsing the main
attack. This is for your inform-
ation only say nothing about
it. Let others speak praise,
not myself.

—*Stonewall Jackson in a letter to his wife
after First Manassas*

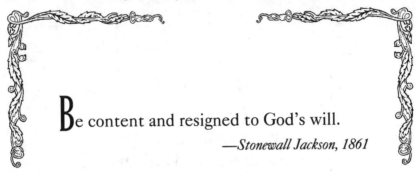

Be content and resigned to God's will.

—*Stonewall Jackson, 1861*

I know that heaven is in store for me, and I should rejoice in the prospect of going there tomorrow. But, still, I am ready to leave it any day . . . for that heaven which I know awaits me . . . I would not agree to the slightest diminution of one shade of my glory there, not for all the fame which I have acquired, or shall ever win in this world.

—*Stonewall Jackson, 1862*

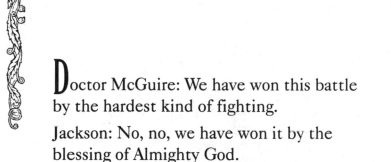

Doctor McGuire: We have won this battle by the hardest kind of fighting.

Jackson: No, no, we have won it by the blessing of Almighty God.

*—Exchange between Stonewall Jackson and Dr. Hunter McGuire, after Second Manassas, 1862*

We can express the grateful conviction of our mind that God was with us and gave to the victory, and unto His holy name be the praise.

*—Stonewall Jackson to his wife, Anna, after Second Manassas, 1862*

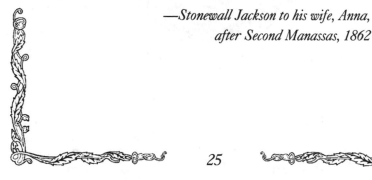

General Hill

# CHAPTER THREE

# Jackson's "Foot" Cavalry

In battle, Jackson commanded with tactical brilliance, living up to his Napoleonic ideals. He tormented the Union forces by keeping them off balance, ordering his troops to strike one part of their line and then another by means of rapid marches. This maneuver gained his soldiers the nickname "foot cavalry."

Even so, Jackson's unkempt appearance and eccentric manner placed him far from the Napoleonic ideal of a dashing leader. Yet, he established a rapport with the common soldier that commanded respect. While insubordinates were harshly reprimanded, the rest of the men, many his former VMI students, dutifully followed his every step, sometimes marching in the stifling heat twenty miles per day, carrying forty to fifty pounds of gear. They worshiped Jackson as the South's hero and showed their admiration with unrelenting support.

This army stays here until the last wounded man is removed. Before I will leave them to the enemy, I will lose many more men.

—*Stonewall Jackson, Winchester, 1862*

Now, gentlemen, let us at once to bed, and see if tomorrow we cannot do something.

—*Stonewall Jackson to his soldiers after a day of profitless marching*

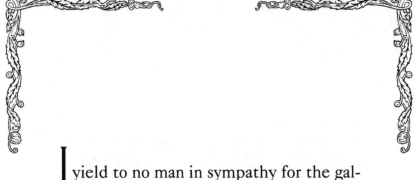

I yield to no man in sympathy for the gallant men under my command; but I am obliged to sweat them tonight, that I may save their blood tomorrow.

—*Stonewall Jackson, 1862*

C harge, men, and yell like furies!

—*Stonewall Jackson to his troops at*
*First Bull Run, July 1861*

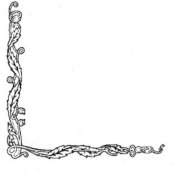

Through the
broad extent of country
over which you have marched,
by your respect for the rights and
property of citizens, you have shown
that you were soldiers not only to
defend, but able and willing
both to defend and
protect.

*—Stonewall Jackson to his troops, 1861*

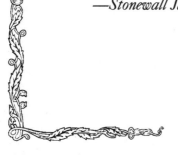

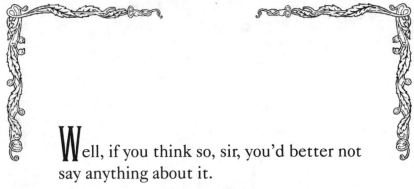

Well, if you think so, sir, you'd better not say anything about it.

*—Stonewall Jackson in response to a fleeing officer*
*at First Manassas who said that the day*
*was going against the Confederates*

Don't say it's impossible! Turn your command over to the next officer. If he can't do it, I'll find someone who can, if I have to take him from the ranks.

*—Stonewall Jackson in his Valley Campaign, 1862*

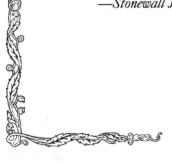

**B**anks is
always ready to
fight, and generally
gets whipped.

*—Stonewall Jackson on his Valley
opponent, Nathaniel P. Banks*

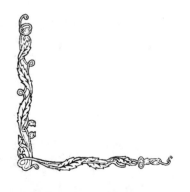
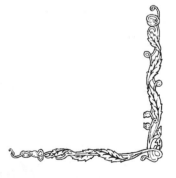

# Who could not conquer with such troops as these?

—*Stonewall Jackson on his march behind Pope's lines at Second Manassas*

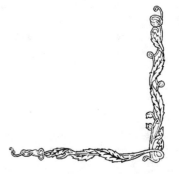

Kyd Douglas: General Hill sends his compliments, sir, and reports that he will probably fail.

Jackson: Go back to General Hill. Tell him if they attack him again he must beat them.

Douglas (later): General Hill presents his compliments and says the attack of the enemy was repulsed.

Jackson: Tell him I knew he would do it.

*—Exchange between General Hill and Stonewall Jackson at Second Manassas*

**W**e will
whip the enemy
but gain no fruits
of victory.

*—Stonewall Jackson to D. H. Hill at
Fredericksburg, 1862*

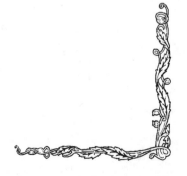

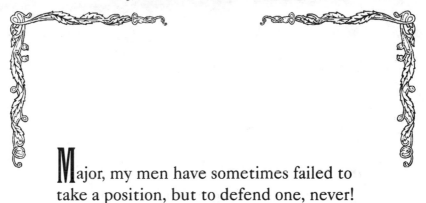

**M**ajor, my men have sometimes failed to take a position, but to defend one, never!

*—Stonewall Jackson to Major Hers von Borcke*
*at Fredericksburg*

**N**ever was there such a chance for cavalry! Oh, that my cavalry were in place!

*—Stonewall Jackson at Front Royal*

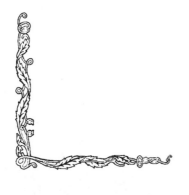

There are but few commanders who properly appreciate the value of celerity.

—*Stonewall Jackson to General Gregg*

The hardships of forced marches are often more painful than the dangers of battle.

—*Stonewall Jackson*

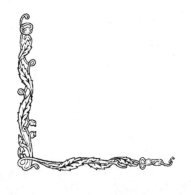
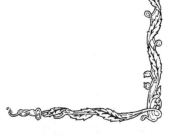

In the Army of
the Shenandoah, you
were the First brigade; in
the Army of the Potomac, you
were the First brigade; you are the
First brigade in the affections of your
general; and I hope in your future
deeds and bearing that you will
be handed down to posterity
as the First brigade in this
our second War of
Independence!

*—Stonewall Jackson's farewell speech
to his troops, November 4, 1861*

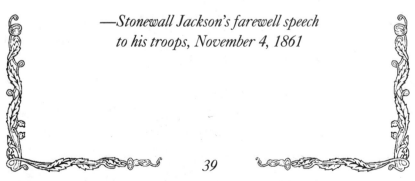

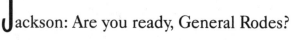

Jackson: Are you ready, General Rodes?

Rodes: Yes, sir.

Jackson: You can go forward then.

> —*Exchange between Stonewall Jackson and
> General Rodes before the famous flank
> assault at Chancellorsville, 1863*

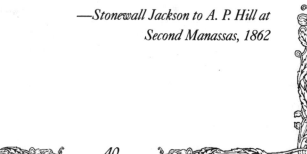

General, your men have done nobly. If you are attacked again, you will beat the enemy back. . . . I'll expect you to beat them!

> —*Stonewall Jackson to A. P. Hill at
> Second Manassas, 1862*

*40*

The danger is
all over. The enemy
is routed! Go back
and tell A. P. Hill to
press forward!

*—Last order given by Stonewall Jackson
in the field, 1863*

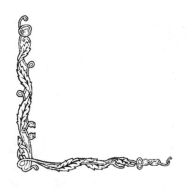
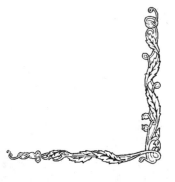

James Longstreet

# CHAPTER FOUR

# Total War

The War Between the States began with the firing on South Carolina's Fort Sumter in April 1861. Three months later, Thomas Jackson and his men became entangled in the invasion of Virginia, as they stood gallantly for the challenge at Bull Run. It was here that Jackson held the enemy against overwhelming odds, earning him the title "Stonewall."

Leading his troops in the Shenandoah Valley, driving the Union soldiers from Winchester, beating Pope at the Second Battle of Bull Run, and crush-

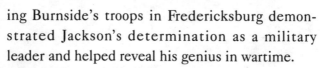

ing Burnside's troops in Fredericksburg demonstrated Jackson's determination as a military leader and helped reveal his genius in wartime.

Even when this strong leader was wounded at the Battle of Chancellorsville, the remaining Southern generals carried on in his spirit. They moved their troops to the heat of battle and valiantly continued to fight.

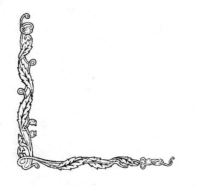

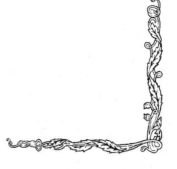

Shoot the
brave officers and
the cowards will run
away and take the
men with them.

*—Stonewall Jackson to Dick Ewell*

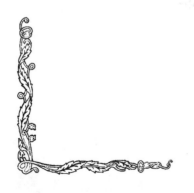

Always mystify, mislead, and surprise the enemy; and when you strike and overcome him, never let up in the pursuit. Never fight against heavy odds if you can hurl your own force on only a part of your enemy and crush it. A small army may thus destroy a large one and repeated victory will make you invincible.

—*Stonewall Jackson*

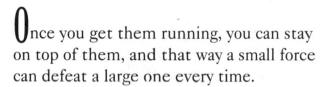

Once you get them running, you can stay on top of them, and that way a small force can defeat a large one every time.

—*Stonewall Jackson*

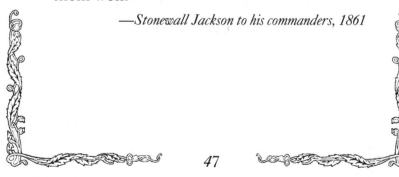

If officers desire to have control over their commands, they must remain habitually with them, industriously attend to their instruction and comfort, and in battle lead them well.

—*Stonewall Jackson to his commanders, 1861*

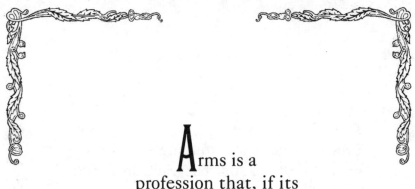

**A**rms is a
profession that, if its
principles are adhered to
for success, requires an officer
do what he fears may be wrong,
and yet, according to military
experience, must be done,
if success is to be
attained.

*—Stonewall Jackson in a letter
to his wife, 1862*

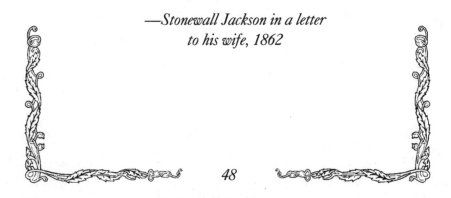

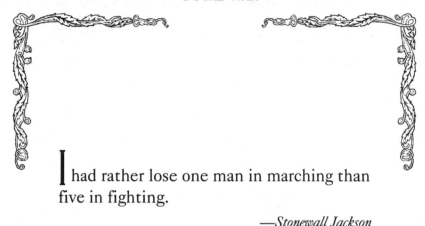

I had rather lose one man in marching than five in fighting.

*—Stonewall Jackson*

To move swiftly, strike vigorously, and secure all the fruits of victory is the secret of a successful war.

*—Stonewall Jackson, 1863*

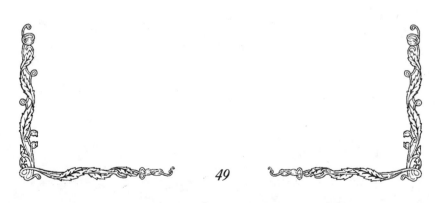

# What is life without honor? Degradation is worse than death.

*—Stonewall Jackson to an officer who had requested leave to visit a sick relative*

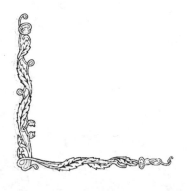
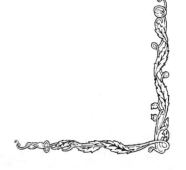

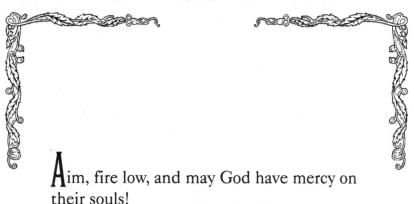

**A**im, fire low, and may God have mercy on their souls!

*—Stonewall Jackson at First Manassas*

**S**ir, we'll give them the bayonet then.

*—Stonewall Jackson in response to an officer's remark about the Federals beating the Confederates back at First Manassas, July 21, 1861*

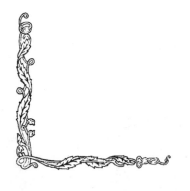
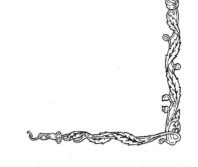

S hoot them all;
I do not wish them
to be brave.

—*Stonewall Jackson, June 1, 1862*

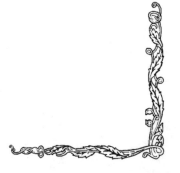

Longstreet: General, do not all those multitudes of Federals frighten you?

Jackson: We shall see very soon whether I shall not frighten *them*.

Longstreet: But, Jackson, what are you going to do with all those people over there?

Jackson: Sir, we shall give them the bayonet.

—*Stonewall Jackson and James Longstreet*
*exchange before Fredericksburg*

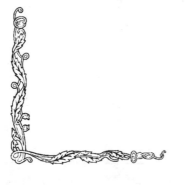

We must do more than defeat their armies. We must destroy them.

—*Stonewall Jackson after Fredericksburg*

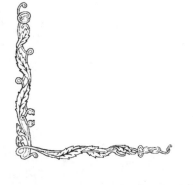

If I can deceive my own friends, I can make certain of deceiving the enemy.

—*Stonewall Jackson on his policy of keeping his thoughts and plans to himself*

# War is the greatest of evils.

*—Stonewall Jackson to Jed Hotchkiss, the former's*
*official map-maker, before Fredericksburg*

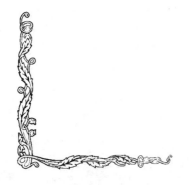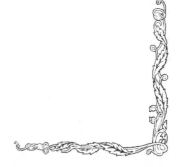

**M**y idea that
the best mode of fighting
is to reserve your fire till the
enemy get or you get them to
close quarters. Then deliver
one deadly, deliberate fire
and charge!

*—Stonewall Jackson after First Manassas*

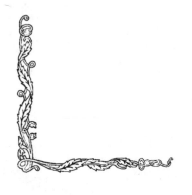
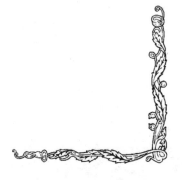

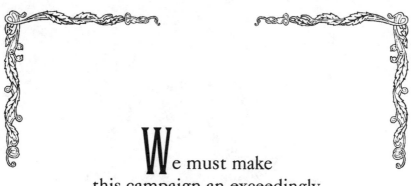

We must make
this campaign an exceedingly
active one. Only thus can a weaker
country cope with a stronger; it must
make up in activity what it lacks in
strength. A defensive campaign can
only be made successful by taking
the aggressive at the
proper time.

*—Stonewall Jackson, 1863*

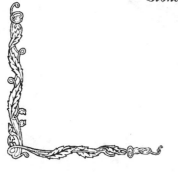

General Robert E. Lee

# CHAPTER FIVE

# Lee and Jackson

Robert E. Lee and Stonewall Jackson were two men who possessed both tactical genius and the belief that God was marching with them. Together, how could they fail? Combining their strengths, Stonewall Jackson became General Robert E. Lee's right-hand man. They formed a model partnership, with Lee directing, and Jackson executing. Working in concert, they led their troops at the Second Battle of Bull Run and Antietam. As the pair moved on to Chancellorsville, the Union army awaited them with twice the manpower. Despite

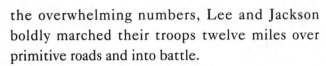

the overwhelming numbers, Lee and Jackson boldly marched their troops twelve miles over primitive roads and into battle.

Jackson's fate was sealed at Chancellorsville. Was Lee's as well? When told the news of Jackson's injury, Lee sent a brief note to his comrade: "You have lost your left arm, I have lost my right." Could he find another such leader to battle by his side whom he could trust as he had Jackson? Though the question pressed heavily on the Confederacy, time alone would reveal the answer.

★ ★ ★

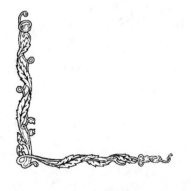

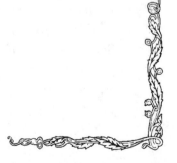

Such an executive officer the sun never shone on. I have but to show him my design, and I know that it can be done, it will be done. . . . Straight as the needle to the pole he advanced to the execution of my purpose.

*—Robert E. Lee on Stonewall Jackson*

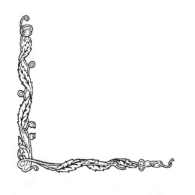
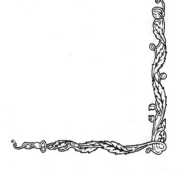

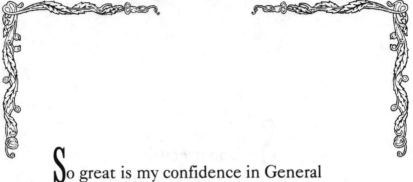

So great is my confidence in General Lee that I am willing to follow him blindfolded.

—*Stonewall Jackson*

We can only act upon probabilities and endeavor to avoid greater evils.

—*Robert E. Lee in a letter to Stonewall Jackson, 1862*

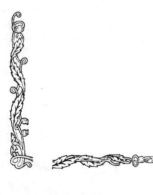
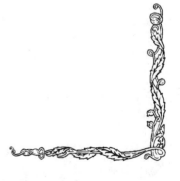

General Lee: How many men will you take?

General Jackson: My whole corps.

General Lee: Well, go on.

>*—Last words exchanged between Robert E. Lee and Stonewall Jackson, Chancellorsville, 1863, when it was decided to risk dividing the Confederate force in a bold flanking march to turn Hooker's right*

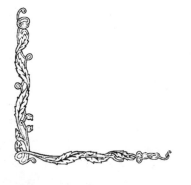
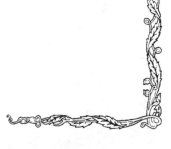

From the opportunities
I had to form a conception of
the character of General Jackson,
I was convinced that he deserved all
of the great confidence in which he
was held by General Lee, and that
was a high honor for anyone.

—*Lafayette McLaws*

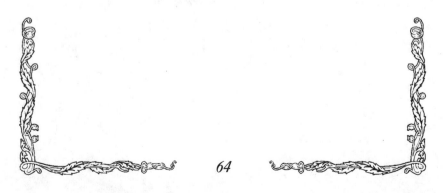

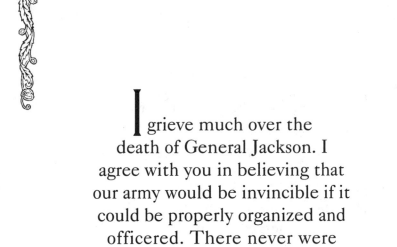

I grieve much over the death of General Jackson. I agree with you in believing that our army would be invincible if it could be properly organized and officered. There never were such men [as Jackson] in an army before.

—*Robert E. Lee*

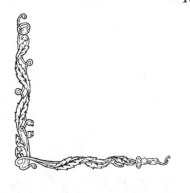

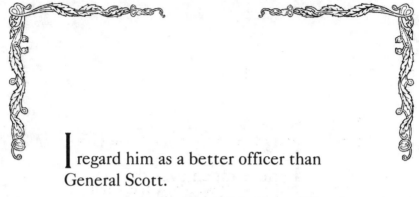

I regard him as a better officer than General Scott.

—*Stonewall Jackson on Robert E. Lee*

General Lee: The fire is heavy. Do you think your men can stand it?

Jackson: They can stand almost anything! They can stand that!

—*Exchange between Stonewall Jackson and Lee during the Seven Days' Campaign*

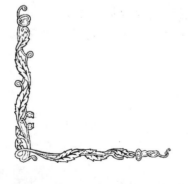

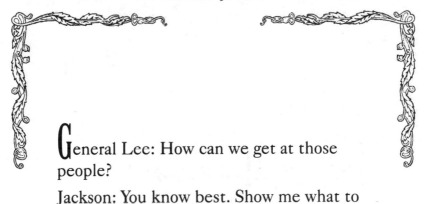

General Lee: How can we get at those people?

Jackson: You know best. Show me what to do, and we will try to do it.

*—Exchange between Stonewall Jackson and*
*Robert E. Lee before Chancellorsville, 1863*

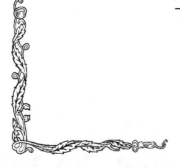

They supplemented each other, and together, with any fair opportunity, they were absolutely invincible.

*—Jefferson Davis on Robert E. Lee*
*and Stonewall Jackson*

My opinion of General Jackson has been greatly enhanced during this expedition. He is true, honest, and brave; has a single eye to the good of the service, and spares no exertion to accomplish his object.

—*Robert E. Lee on Jackson after the Maryland Campaign, 1862*

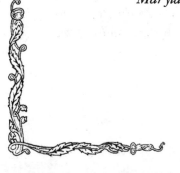

He never failed me. Why, if I had had Stonewall Jackson at Gettysburg, I should have won that battle; and a complete victory would have given us Washington and Baltimore if not Philadelphia, and would have established the independence of the Confederacy.

—*Robert E. Lee speaking after the war*

Could I have chosen for the good of the country to be disabled in your stead.

—*Robert E. Lee to Stonewall Jackson*
*shortly after his wounding*

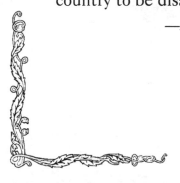

John Bell Hood

# CHAPTER SIX

# Contemporaries in Blue and Gray

The name "Stonewall Jackson" inspired fear in Yankee soldiers. How does one defeat a mythic general who is larger than life? Union leaders dreaded his approach in any skirmish; they knew of his wily, fast-moving tactics, which accounted for his successes in previous battles. Their trepidation, however, was matched by their respect, which many Union soldiers expressed after learning of his demise.

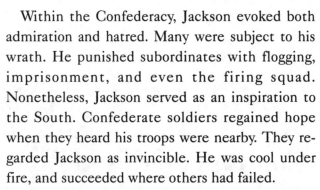

Within the Confederacy, Jackson evoked both admiration and hatred. Many were subject to his wrath. He punished subordinates with flogging, imprisonment, and even the firing squad. Nonetheless, Jackson served as an inspiration to the South. Confederate soldiers regained hope when they heard his troops were nearby. They regarded Jackson as invincible. He was cool under fire, and succeeded where others had failed.

The soldiers' deep respect was evident in their jokes about Jackson's unorthodox entrance into heaven: The angels came down to get him and searched everywhere. Unsuccessful, they returned to heaven, only to find that the general had made a flank march and reached heaven ahead of them.

★ ★ ★

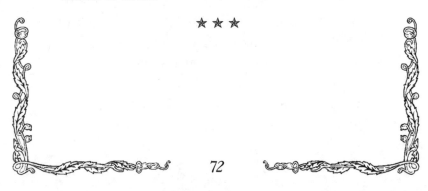

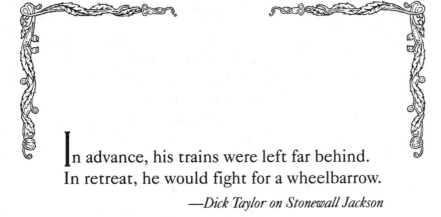

In advance, his trains were left far behind. In retreat, he would fight for a wheelbarrow.

—*Dick Taylor on Stonewall Jackson*

I pray that God may spare him to us to see us through. If General Lee had Grant's resources, he would soon end the war; but Old Jack can do it without resources.

—*General George Pickett in a letter to his wife on Stonewall Jackson*

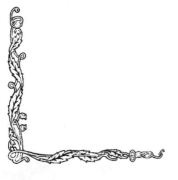

**O**ld Jackson is no fool.
He knows how to keep his
own counsel, and does curious
things, but he has a method
in his madness.

—*R. S. Ewell after the battles of*
*Port Republic and Cross Keys*

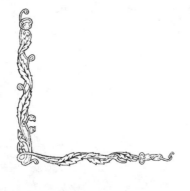
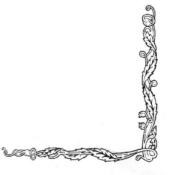

Jackson would
not have hesitated when
he saw the chance of success
offered by the evident confusion
of the retreating foe, but would have
gone forward, with his characteristic
dash and daring, and these im-
portant positions would have
doubtless been ours.

*—Lafayette McLaws on the first day
at Gettysburg*

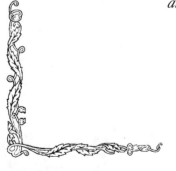

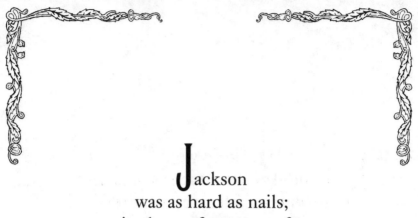

Jackson
was as hard as nails;
in the performance of a
duty he always was. I never
knew him in such a cast to
temper justice with mercy;
his very words were
merciless.

—*Lieutenant Henry Kyd Douglas on*
*Stonewall Jackson*

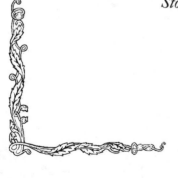

76

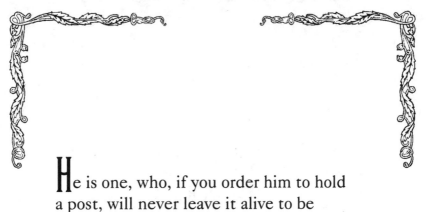

He is one, who, if you order him to hold
a post, will never leave it alive to be
occupied by the enemy.

*—Anonymous quote on Stonewall Jackson*

He is dead. Who can fill his place?

*—General Richard B. Garnett on*
*Stonewall Jackson's death*

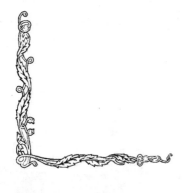

I don't like
Jackson's movements;
he will suddenly appear
when least expected.

—*General McClellan to General Halleck
before Second Manassas, 1862*

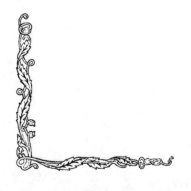

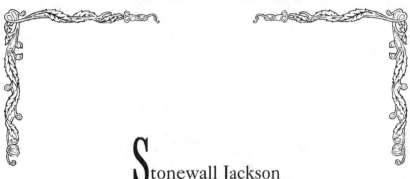

Stonewall Jackson was victorious. Even his enemies praise him, but providentially for us, it was the last battle he waged against the American Union.

*—General Oliver Otis Howard, commander of the XI Corps at Chancellorsville and victim of Jackson's famous flank attack, speaking after the war*

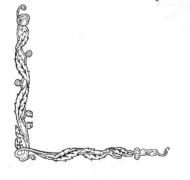
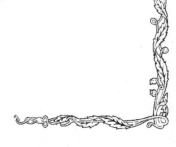

J. E. B. Stuart

# CHAPTER SEVEN

# Untimely Death

The Battle of Chancellorsville proved to be more than just another struggle. It shattered a legendary war hero, along with the hopes of the South.

As Jackson and a few comrades rode from the woods after inspecting the battle site, his troops opened fire, thinking they were Union soldiers. With Jackson wounded and the Confederate position exposed, the battle raged that night. A week later, the news of Jackson's death ricocheted down the lines of his fighting men like a bullet, spreading a dark cloud over the already-bloody battlefield. His soldiers grieved; the South grieved. Even

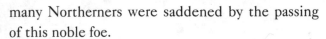

many Northerners were saddened by the passing of this noble foe.

What would have happened if Jackson had lived? Would he have been the savior the Confederates needed? Could this legendary commander have led them to a final victory? The questions about the fate of the Confederacy live on, as do their debatable answers. In his own words, Stonewall Jackson might have replied: "Be content and resigned to God's will."

★ ★ ★

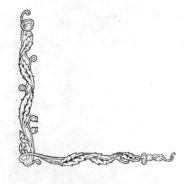

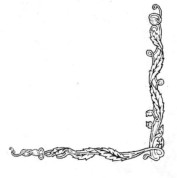

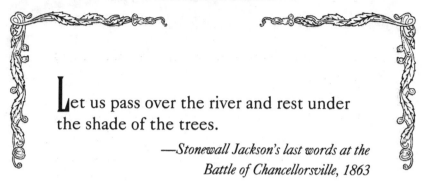

Let us pass over the river and rest under the shade of the trees.

*—Stonewall Jackson's last words at the
Battle of Chancellorsville, 1863*

Ah, Captain, any victory is dearly bought which deprives us of the services of General Jackson, even for a short time.

*—Robert E. Lee to Captain Wilbourne, one of Stonewall
Jackson's aides, on the wounding of Jackson*

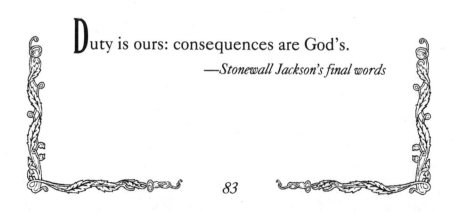

Duty is ours: consequences are God's.

*—Stonewall Jackson's final words*

**I**t is the Lord's Day. My wish is fulfilled. I have always desired to die on Sunday.

> —*Stonewall Jackson, May 10, 1863,*
> *to Alexander Pendleton*

**A** national calamity has befallen us.

> —*President Jefferson Davis on the death*
> *of Stonewall Jackson*

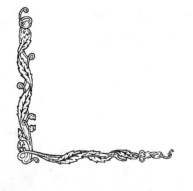
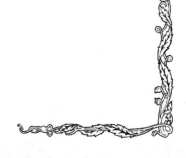

I am not afraid to die.
I am willing to abide by the
will of my Heavenly Father. But
I do not believe I shall die at this
time. I am persuaded the Almighty has yet a work
for me to perform.

*—Thomas J. Jackson just before his death, 1863*

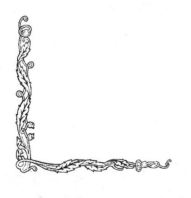
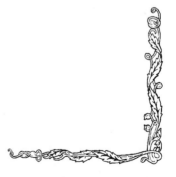

I regret to inform you that the great and good Jackson is no more. He died at 3:15 p.m. of pneumonia, calm, serene and happy. May his spirit pervade our whole army; our country will then be secure.

—*Robert E. Lee to J. E. B. Stuart*

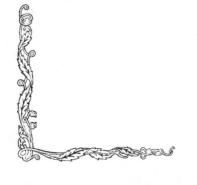

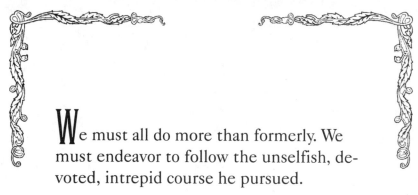

We must all do more than formerly. We must endeavor to follow the unselfish, devoted, intrepid course he pursued.

*—Robert E. Lee to John Bell Hood on*
*Stonewall Jackson's death*

Surely General Jackson must recover. God will not take him from us, now that we need him so much. Surely he will be spared to us, in answer to the many prayers which are offered him.

*—Robert E. Lee before Stonewall Jackson's death*

ISBN 1-888952-36-9

6   10529 00048   3